25+1

Rebecca Fearnley

BookLeaf
Publishing

Presentation by *BookLeaf Publishing*

Web: www.bookleafpub.com

E-mail: info@bookleafpub.com

ISBN: 9789395621250

First edition 2022

DEDICATION

For all 20-something-year-olds alike. You are not alone, we can do it together x

ACKNOWLEDGEMENT

Beth, thank you for encouraging me to go for it.
XO
Ry & Teegs, thank you for being my
cheerleaders always. XO

social expectations suffocate us
clips our wings and grounds us
strips us of our individuality, our uniqueness
cripples us if we make mistakes
and shames us if we fail

but the beauty of humanity is that no bud
blossoms in the same way

so break those damn boxes

and bloom shamelessly
and beautifully
just as you were always meant to.

a smile is more than just a smile

its value knows no bounds
in its purest form it is sunshine
beaming from the soul
shining a light on those
who need it
who value its sincerity
who cherish its warmth
who feel safe when they see it.

If you do one thing today,
put a smile on.

31/07

today I look upon the limitless horizon
climb a mountain
stand on its peak
bask in the sunshine
fill my lungs with air brimming with pride

little girls everywhere adjusting their crowns and
putting their England shirts and boots on, ready
for takedown.

It is time girls -
your future is bright
It is time to fight the good fight.

if "hope" is a thing with feathers
anxiety is the bitch who broke her wings.

5

be thankful for:
coffee
sunshine
rainbows
boys who don't text you back

the universe works in mysterious ways
be grateful
always x

Oh, mother nature!
The bitch arrives and she says:
"Why, hello old friend!"

#whatarelief - rebecca fearnley

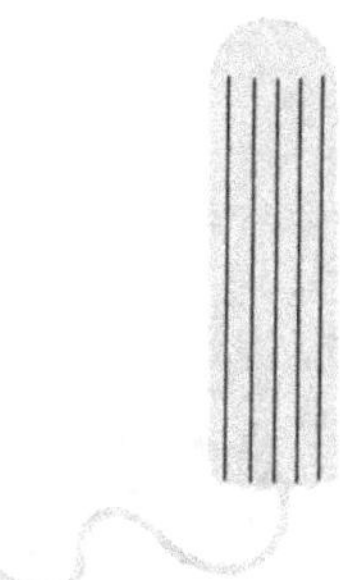

At what point do we grow up and no longer think we are bangin'?

my worthiness is not determined by my thick
thighs or jean size
nor is it determined by the number of men who
want to get in them

my worthiness has always and will always be
determined only by me, myself, and I.

My most precious moments
are the ones where I
drown out anxiety
with joy
and music
and love
and laughter
and margaritas

an ode to the vag x

the vulva, don't pull the:
"it's just a vagina"
she is the connection
between the uterus
and the numerous
men who want to find uranus.
she stretches, she collapses, she retracts
but she is more than just her acts
she self-lubricates and medicates
and has some hard-to-reach associates
she is both a barrier and an access
but we digress

from her very first menarche, we possess
the ability to bless
(with much success)
the world full of life
with the help of a midwife
and occasionally a knife.
she is supported by her pleasure-seeking
sidekick –
clit –
who doesn't give a shit
if you can't quite find it

she grows a little
looks like a shiny red skittle
remove her hood
to reveal the lovebud,
but the unlikelihood
of you locating her womanhood
is about as great as your softwood.
but don't worry sweet guy
we've had centuries of only inner thigh
it is a good job we can self-satisfy.

sometimes id rather the ground swallow me
whole
into the upside down, a black hole, or to where
all the missing things go.
i feel detached - unlatched - snatched from
reality
i neither feel seen nor heard.

sometimes i want to sit in the pub alone
drink beers and sing through tears, or dance on
broken glass and shake my ass.
i feel elated - invigorated - electrified by
carelessness
i am both seen and heard.

both of these versions are still me.
both of these versions are ok.

don't worry - i've got you - we are all a little
broken.
don't you know?
all the best things are.

brothers

it is great to be born with a ready-made best
friend
an absolute godsend
on whom you depend
yet will defend until the bitter end
a person from whom you descend
and intend to tie every loose end

nature vs nurture will be a debate
which will continue to frustrate

but to defy all odds - we are the same person
despite the gods and our squads -
we are two peas in a pod

So lets just appreciate
how lucky am I
to have a guy
like you Ry.

anxious annie sucks x

numbness
to protect
extinguishing
joy
and
leaving me
amongst the darkness
lost in the fog
unable to think
questioning my validity
relevance
purpose
avoiding humanity
for
fear
of
embarrassment
left tired
fatigued
staring
at a reflection
unrecognisable
eyes
dim
dull

despondent
lost in it
consumed by it

13

soul sucked out of a sunset
transformed into reels with "feels
like summer" steals the realness,
idealness of the moment

a beautiful life is not one with a
carefully curated online presence

numpties more invested in the strength
of the wifi - as their life travels right by

honey, put your phone down
every once in a while

that sunset will shine brighter
be more beautiful
than any prizefighter
that any tiny camera
or Paris filter will capture.

#dontjustlivelifeforthegram

tequila is sunshine in a bottle
she makes you feel warm and fuzzy
invincible and sexy
she brings the life and soul to any party
just as long as you bring the salt.

but tomorrow she will leave,
as quickly as she appeared
abandoning you
leaving you to mope with anxious annie
and drown in your salty tears.

beer fear - rebecca fearnley

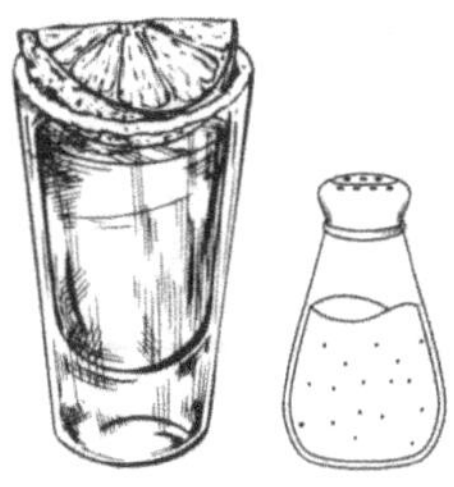

15

words can take you anywhere
travel to different lands
magical lands
live a life you could merely dream of
connect with characters
love them
champion them
empathise and feel for them

words can help you
heal and reflect on your own character
in your very own story

drugs might
temporarily
help you to
avoid life's problems

words will help you deal with them.

#drugsarenttheanswer
#booksoverfucks
#escapism

friends

I've got tall ones
I've got small ones
I've got much older and wise ones
I've got new ones
I've got male ones
I've got pale ones
I've got frail ones
I've got some high-maintenance ones

I've let some go along the way
shed them like the seasons
but I have some who know too much shit
that I dare not split

but the best ones are the ones
who make your world sparkle
they are your torch in the night
a hand to hold tight
when the tide gets rough
sure enough, they reassure you
you are made of hard stuff
and they instantly turn your heart to mush.

17

in a world full of Kim Kardashians
be more Rupi Kaur.

18

validation isn't required
it isn't awarded
and it isn't achieved

compliments are great
but they aren't
necessary

to deny yourself validation
and believe you are anything
but beautiful is foolish and cruel

your beauty within will shine
farther and wider once you
find it.

you won't need to look hard
it will be right there
next to your heart x

19

"but miss, why?"
a childs curiosity knows no bounds
their sweet sounds and innocence
wonder why I live my life such as I

and I say:
I follow my giant heart
from the very start
I do what feels right.
however scary or slight
I reflect on who I am
breathe deeply into my diaphragm
I make mistakes and fall
and sometimes I feel small,
but most of all
I chase change and challenge
stay true to my values
practice gratitude.
find goodness within everybody
magnetise and embody,
accept what isn't meant for me
rid myself of bad energy -
I am loud and proud
stand tall amongst a crowd
I am colourful and controversial

cheerful and tearful.
I practice forgiveness
and I try to forget
but most importantly, I love always.
even when deeply exposed
and vulnerable
my giant heart leads me down my next path
and the universe has got my back.

find happiness in the small things.
the sun will rise and life will surprise you.